OCEAN CITY TALES

Ocean City Tales: Sharklock Bones Beach Towns

In the Sharklock Bones Detective Agency office

MIKE HAMMER: So, Sharklock, did Data and I do a good job for you in Cape May?

MIKE HAMMER, DETECTIVE

SHARKLOCK BONES: Yes, you did well. However, I did talk with Dr. Flotsam, my associate and we feel you must be a little more aggressive in the future. It's our opinion that with the combination of your brawn and Data's brain, you two will make a great detective duo! During your last mission in Cape May, you seemed to get spooked easily. Remember, you are a hammerhead shark, one of the fastest and most agile of the shark world. You also have spectacular panoramic vision with those great eyes. You have no reason at all to be afraid of anything, so stop acting like the Cowardly Lionfish from the Wizard of Aaahs.

THE STUDIOUS DATA DOLPHIN

That being said, we think you are ready for another assignment if you want it.

DATA DOLPHIN: Just tell us where to go and what we must do.

SHARKLOCK BONES: A beach town called Ocean City. Have you heard of it?

DATA DOLPHIN: The New Jersey one or the Maryland one?

SHARKLOCK BONES: You're right as usual. It's the New Jersey one. It's well known as America's Greatest Family Resort, so take an extra day to enjoy the sights.

Now, your assignment is to check out the wreck of the Sindia, especially in the hull of the ship. Data, do you know of this wreck?

DATA DOLPHIN: The Sindia was built in Belfast, Ireland by a company called Harland and Wolff in 1887. This was the same company that later built the so-called unsinkable ship, the Titanic. The Sindia was one of the last commercial sailing ships. This was before steam-powered ships took over. It was purchased in 1900 by John D. Rockefeller's company...

MODEL OF SINDIA IN OCEAN CITY HISTORICAL MUSEUM

SHARKLOCK: Data, focus!! We're interested in the wreck, not the entire history of the ship. Our agency has been hired to check out the wreck, if possible, to try to determine if the Sindia indeed had a golden Buddha hidden away in its hold.

MIKE HAMMER: The Sindia sunk on December 15, 1901. Wouldn't someone have found it by now? It's 115 years later.

SHARKLOCK: The wreck is between 16th and 17th Street in Ocean City. Some of the homeowners want this put to rest as treasure hunters to this day come to look for the Buddha. The treasure seekers use up parking spots, leave litter and trash behind.

The Sindia was over 300 feet long and had a steel hull. It was finalizing a 10,000-mile voyage from Kobe, Japan to New York City when it was hit by a winter gale off the coast of Cape May. It was buffeted for four days and finally ran aground broadside on the Ocean City beach.

The steel hull and the ballast of 1200 tons of manganese stone acted as a wedge into the shifting sands. The hull cracked open and the hold filled with more sand and water.

Over the years, between further sinking and beach replenishment projects, the Sindia disappeared from sight.

MIKE HAMMER: But why hire us?

SHARKLOCK: Have you noticed? We're fish; we can dive without air breathing apparatus. Human divers are not allowed near the wreck. It's too dangerous.

DATA DOLPHIN: Ahem! Remember me? Dolphins are mammals. We breathe air!

SHARKLOCK: OK, but we can work something out for you. Now, get moving, you two!

On the beach at Corson's Inlet

MIKE HAMMER: Whew, Data, I'm bushed. Let's rest on this beach.

DATA DOLPHIN: But we only have a few more miles to go! Ocean City is just north of here.

MIKE HAMMER: Let's just get our breath now. But wait a minute! That dark spot on the beach is moving quickly. I don't know what it is, but I'm plenty scared. Back in the drink we go!

DATA DOLPHIN: They're just crabs, small crabs. They live in the sand and are more scared of us than we should be of them.

MIKE HAMMER: There's thousands of them, Data! What? They're disappearing before my eyes.

DATA DOLPHIN: These little crabs are completely harmless and went into hiding under the sand to get away from us.

MIKE HAMMER: Skittery little buggers, aren't they? You know, Data, it's very nice and peaceful here.

DATA DOLPHIN: Corson's Inlet is a state park covering over 340 acres. It's one of the last undeveloped sections of oceanfront property in New Jersey. The inlet separates Ocean City from Strathmere, New Jersey.

A famous poet named Archie Ammons loved to visit here and found it very relaxing. He wrote a poem about it called "Corson's Inlet" in 1967.

CORSON'S INLET ADJOINS OCEAN CITY

MIKE HAMMER: Okay, time to get moving. Next stop, the Ocean City Boardwalk.

On the boardwalk

MIKE HAMMER: Data, this certainly is a nice boardwalk. Oh, no! Watch out. There's a pirate ship up there with a giant parrot. The ship's cannon just fired. Let's take cover, quickly!

DATA DOLPHIN: You really must calm down. Remember what your cousin, Sharklock, said. You must stop being afraid of everything.

MIKE HAMMER: Data, you numbskull, we were just fired upon by a pirate ship! Aren't you afraid?

CASTAWAY COVE

DATA DOLPHIN: Of course not. Stop running away and look again. It's on top of a boardwalk amusement park called Playland's Castaway Cove. Nothing to worry about. Did you know this boardwalk was first built in 1880? Due to fires and storms, it has been rebuilt a few times and is a world famous boardwalk.

MIKE HAMMER: So this is the oldest boardwalk?

DATA DOLPHIN: No, not quite. That title belongs to Atlantic City. Boardwalks were built to prevent tourists from bringing sand into the hotels and casinos.

Ocean City was originally called Peck's Beach after a whaler who had a camp here back in 1770.

MIKE HAMMER: But look at that hotel a few blocks down! It has giant fish and seahorses on the side of it climbing toward the top. Data, we need to get out of town now! It's way too spooky.

DATA DOLPHIN: Mike, please calm down! That's the Flanders Hotel. It's been there since the 1920's. The fish you see are part of the construction, similar to the gargoyles on buildings in Europe.

MIKE HAMMER: Well, I'm bushed. Should we spend the night at the Flanders?

DATA DOLPHIN: Just so you know, the Flanders is supposedly haunted by a ghost named Emily. She's called the Lady in White.

MIKE HAMMER: In that case, I'm not staying there for love nor money.

SCARY CREATURES OR DECORATIONS?

FLANDERS HOTEL ENTRANCE

DATA DOLPHIN: I believe I'll stay at the Flanders overnight.

MIKE HAMMER: But aren't you worried about the Lady in White?

DATA DOPHIN: Emily is supposedly a happy ghost if she exists at all. No one has ever been hurt by her and she supposedly also sings. I'm not worried in the least.

MIKE HAMMER: I'll stay over at Watson's Regency. They have an indoor pool and spa to soothe my aching muscles (and no ghost!). It was a long swim here from Fishtown.

DATA DOLPHIN: Mike, Sharklock warned you about not facing your fears. You're constantly avoiding things that scare you, but shouldn't. There's no evidence that Emily, the Lady in White, ever hurt anyone.

FLANDERS LOBBY- LADY IN WHITE?

MIKE HAMMER: Well, alright, I'll stay at the Flanders then. But if the Lady in White does me harm, it's on you, Data!

FLANDERS LOBBY

The next morning on the boardwalk

DATA DOLPHIN: So how did you sleep?

MIKE HAMMER: Not too bad considering the racket around midnight out in the hallway.

DATA DOLPHIN: Racket? What racket?

MIKE HAMMER: Around midnight, some lady kept singing and walking up and down the corridor.

DATA DOLPHIN: Did you see her?

MIKE HAMMER: Sure did. She was very pretty and had on a white shimmery dress. Really great voice. Then I went back to bed and slept fine. Why?

DATA DOLPHIN: That was Emily, the ghost, the Lady in White. Weren't you afraid? You're scared of everything, it seems!

MIKE HAMMER: Ghost? Nah, she was laughing and singing. Couldn't have been a ghost, sorry.

DATA DOLPHIN: (*sigh!*) Never mind. Before we take a dip, let's walk down the Boardwalk.

MIKE HAMMER: What's this great building here at 8th Street and the Boardwalk?

DATA DOLPHIN: This is the Ocean City Music Pier. It's been here since 1928. It provides space for public and private concerts and orchestrated events. It's home to the Miss New Jersey Pageant and also the Ocean City Pops.

We'd better hustle up to 17th. It's starting to cloud up.

OCEAN CITY MUSIC PIER

Boardwalk at 17th Street

MIKE HAMMER: Okay, Data, you seem suited up with your gear. Let's get to it. We have to find what's left of the Sindia's wreck and go inside.

DATA DOLPHIN: I don't like the looks of that sky. It looks like a storm is rolling in.

MIKE HAMMER: Now who's scared? We'll both be in the water. What could go wrong?

DATA DOLPHIN: Remember, I'm a mammal. Sharklock gave me this SCUBA setup to wear in case we're down there too long. But, again, that storm looks pretty threatening.

Splash!

MIKE HAMMER: It appears between the shifting sands and the Army Corps of Engineers constantly replenishing the beachfront with new sand that the wreck of the Sindia is barely a bump on the ocean floor.

SINDIA RUN AGROUND (courtesy of the Ocean City Historical Museum)

DATA DOLPHIN: But I can see an opening where one of the masts broke off. We can get down to the hold from there.

MIKE HAMMER: Tight squeeze, but we can do it. Let's go.

DATA DOLPHIN: My SCUBA equipment has this flashlight so we can see in here. That storm above is pretty fierce. This old wreck seems to be moving back and forth. Look, you can see the giant crack in the iron hull. Remind me, just what are we looking for?

SINDIA ARTIFACTS (courtesy of the Ocean City Historical Museum)

MIKE HAMMER: A large golden Buddha and dog statues made of jade. According to legend, many items looted from Buddhist temples during the Boxer Rebellion of 1900 found their way onto Rockefeller's ship in Kobe, Japan. None of these treasures were listed on the ship's manifest, but it did list 200 tons of manganese ore that was stored in crates as ballast.

DATA DOLPHIN: It's quite claustrophobic in here. The sand is swirling and shifting against the port side of the hull. It's coming in through the busted seam in the hull and what remains of the ship is listing badly. If this storm gets worse, it will collapse on its side.

MIKE HAMMER: With us inside! The timbers are creaking and the waves are cracking the sides of the ship. Let's get out of here now!

DATA DOLPHIN: My air hose is caught on this spar and the sand is tumbling over me. I can't move. Get out, Mike. Save yourself. I'm done for.

MIKE HAMMER: There's no way I'd desert you, Data. You seem to forget, I'm one of the toughest fish in this ocean. I'll get you out of this or we'll perish together, my old friend.

DATA DOLPHIN: Your tail is really powerful. Swing it over the sand pile on my body to loosen the sand. Plus your hammerhead is really flexible, maybe it can free this air hose.

MIKE HAMMER: There we go. Can you move around now? This whole room is collapsing around us.

DATA DOLPHIN: When my air hose was knocked free, it ripped. I'm inhaling water and almost out of air. The escape opening is now covered with sand. I'll never make it. Leave me!

SINDIA BEFORE THE STORM

AFTER STORM

(both pictures courtesy of the Ocean City Historical Museum)

MIKE HAMMER: Just keep holding your breath and hang onto me as tight as you can. I'm going to smash through the wooden side of the ship and get you out of here.

DATA DOLPHIN: But that's impossible. Just go, save yourself.

MIKE HAMMER: Hang on for your life, Data. Here we go!

Crash!

MIKE HAMMER: Almost at the surface now. The Sindia is done for, I'm afraid. But you're not. Inhale now! We're up on the surface again, but the waves are pretty rough. I'll pull both of us to shore.

I'm not sure how to let Sharklock know that we failed in our mission.

DATA DOLPHIN: (gasp!) We didn't fail, Mike. There was no treasure down there.

MIKE HAMMER: It was probably covered with sand.

DATA DOLPHIN: No. In the days following the wreck, a series of tugboats and barges showed up at the site of the wreck. They were sent from New York harbor by John D. Rockefeller to salvage whatever they could. It was reported their longshoremen removed most if not all the crates in the hull.

MIKE HAMMER: The crates were filled with manganese ore.

DATA DOLPHIN: Manganese ore is close to worthless and, if used for ballast, it's just poured into the hull. It's not crated!

MIKE HAMMER: So you think the crates contained the treasures?

DATA DOLPHIN: Of course they did. Why else would Rockefeller send all the men and boats down here?

MIKE HAMMER: Fascinating. How did you learn about all of this?

DATA DOLPHIN: I visited the Ocean City Historical Museum this morning while you were still asleep. They have a large display of artifacts from the Sindia and all the news articles from that time. The answer is rather obvious. No treasure left!

SINDIA DISPLAY AT THE OCEAN CITY HISTORICAL MUSEUM

MIKE HAMMER: I'll let Sharklock know. Maybe the neighbors along these streets can post signs to keep the treasure seekers at bay.

DATA DOLPHIN: There's nothing left of the Sindia after you crashed through the side and the storm damaged the wreck further.

MIKE HAMMER: So the treasure seekers will no longer bother the neighbors!

DATA DOLPHIN: I feel you're wrong. The legend of the Sindia treasure has been around for over a century. Like most legends, it will still be around in another hundred years and more. Treasure seekers will continue to be around.

MIKE HAMMER: You know, we sure had a close call back there.

DATA DOLPHIN: You saved my life! I couldn't believe how brave you were. And after all the times you've been afraid since we left Fishtown, you still came through for me! Sharklock was right. You shouldn't be in fear of anything!

MIKE HAMMER: We're here on the beach now. Let's head up to the Boardwalk. And you're right, Data. From now on, I will no longer be afraid of anything! Nothing can scare me again. I am one rough tough shark.

MIKE HAMMER, ONE ROUGH TOUGH SHARK

Wait a second! Run, Data! There's a giant gorilla on the Boardwalk. He's bigger than King Kong! He'll eat us! Hide!

DATA DOLPHIN: (*sigh!*) No, Mike, that's just the prop statue for Congo Falls Miniature Golf. Don't worry, I won't tell Sharklock.

CONGO FALLS MINI-GOLF

DUSK IN OCEAN CITY

Made in the USA
Middletown, DE
03 July 2016